Deep Dive

Teaching Tips

Orange Level 6

This book focuses on the phonemes **/i_e/ie/**.

Before Reading

- Discuss the title. Ask readers what they think the book will be about. Have them briefly explain why.
- Ask readers to name the missing letter for each word on page 3. What do they notice about the "i" sound in these words? Is the "i" a long or short vowel in each?

Read the Book

- Encourage readers to break down unfamiliar words into units of sound. Then, ask them to string the sounds together to create the words.
- Urge readers to point out when the focused phonics phonemes appear in the text.

After Reading

- Encourage children to reread the book independently or with a friend.
- Ask readers to name other words with /i_e/ or /ie/ phonemes. On a separate sheet of paper, have them write the words out.

© 2024 Booklife Publishing
This edition is published by arrangement with Booklife Publishing.

North American adaptations © 2024 Jump!
5357 Penn Avenue South
Minneapolis, MN 55419
www.jumplibrary.com

Decodables by Jump! are published by Jump! Library.
All rights reserved. No part of this book may be reproduced in any form without written permission from the publisher.

Library of Congress Cataloging-in-Publication Data is available at www.loc.gov or upon request from the publisher.

ISBN: 979-8-88996-855-9 (hardcover)
ISBN: 979-8-88996-856-6 (paperback)
ISBN: 979-8-88996-857-3 (ebook)

Photo Credits

Images are courtesy of Shutterstock.com. With thanks to Getty Images, Thinkstock Photo and iStockphoto. Cover – dibrova. 2–3 – Photoonlife, Eric Isselee, My Sunnyday, bestv. 4–5 – ChameleonsEye, Max Topchii, Richard Whitcombe. 6–7 – Photos BrianScantlebury, Stas Moroz. 8–9 – U.S. Navy photo by Mass Communication Specialist 2nd Class Justin Stumberg, Public domain, via Wikimedia Commons, Widhibek. 10–11 – Dudarev Mikhail, Rich Carey. 12–13 – frantisekhojdysz, Lillac. 14–15 – VisionDive. 16 – Shutterstock.

Can you fill in the gaps?

ti_e

mi_e

pi_e

sli_e

Have you ever tried to dive? That is when you go down deep in the sea.

Divers can see sea life under the water. They have to look out for things with spikes that can sting, such as sea urchins and starfish.

Crown-of-thorns starfish

Some divers can go deep, deep down. Air in tanks keeps them alive.

First, divers get dressed in their gear.
They connect their air tanks with a pipe.
They check it all a few times to be safe.

Then, they ride a boat to a good spot to dive. To get off the boat in a deep spot, they do a stride dive and just step off the boat.

Stride dive

They can do a back roll from the boat when they are in a spot that is not deep.

Back roll

Divers cannot speak or hear under the sea.

To say something, divers need their hands. A ring with three fingers up tells people they are fine.

Sunlight cannot reach deep under the sea. It is quite dark. Divers bring lights with them that can shine under the water.

Dive light

In order to be safe, divers take a long time to come up from the sea.

Divers can look for sharks under the sea. They stay inside a metal cage with thick bars so that they do not get hurt.

The sharks cannot bite them there.

Point to the objects that have /i_e/ in their name.